The Stuff That Fun Is Made Of

A COMPREHENSIVE COLLECTION OF RECIPES FOR PLAY AND LEARNING

SELENA LAPORTE

Emerald Books

P.O. BOX 635
LYNNWOOD, WA 98046

This book is dedicated to all the parents and teachers who have searched through many books to find that one recipe that worked and to my loving family who endured our kitchen being turned into a testing lab.

Acknowledgments

I would like to thank my mom, Renee, for her ideas, constructive criticism, and help with editing. This book would not have been possible without her. I want to thank my children, Marshall and Bailey, for their patience and for being my best testers and critics, and my husband, Chad, for being there and believing in me.

Contents

EDIBLE PLAY DOUGH

LANDSCAPE AND RELIEF MAP DOUGH

PART 2: PAINTS

BRUSH PAINT

FINGER PAINT

FACE PAINT

INK-TYPE PAINT

EDIBLE FINGER PAINTS

OTHER PAINTS

PART 3: PASTES AND GLUES

PASTES

GLUES

PART 4: OTHER FUN STUFF

SAND CONCOCTIONS

SENSORY RECIPES FOR FUN

BUBBLES

PAPER-MACHE

WHERE TO FIND INGREDIENTS

Preface

I believe this book is the greatest collection of fun recipes available for children today. I spent countless hours testing each recipe until I felt that it was reliable and would offer children and students the greatest enjoyment possible. Some of the recipes are classics, some I concocted after a failed testing, while others came as an inspiration. On one occasion I felt the urge to make my own play dough recipe. I had realized that none of the recipes I had run across were geared for the child who might be allergic to wheat products. In the preschool where I worked, several children suffered from wheat allergies. That situation inspired me to work diligently in my kitchen with a bag of oat flour until I had a nice pliable oat dough those children could use.

During my research, I discovered that many of the recipes I tried did not work—like the time I tested some crystal goo that was supposed to be used for modeling crystal stones. At first when I tested it, I thought maybe I wasn't mixing it correctly because the glue turned into rubber and the rock salt just sat there. I retested it, doing so very precisely, but it fell apart in my hands, and the glue turned to rubber once more. And as for modeling, I can say the only modeling this recipe did was in my trash can!

Parents, teachers, and children often experience this type of disappointment. When we open a book that offers instruction, we expect it to be accurate, informative, and, of course, to work right.

My vision was to compile into one book a variety of fun concoctions that really work. Each recipe in this book has been personally tested by me and my five-year-old son, Bailey. Each offers a learning experience such as measuring, cutting, experimenting, exploration, and creativity. But most importantly, my sons say that these recipes are a lot of fun to make. Bailey, my youngest son, often joined me in the kitchen while I was working and would beg me to make more play doughs. We both found it quite hilarious when I thought of the idea to create a play dough out of instant baby cereal. When I added one cup of water to one cup of baby cereal, I obviously had forgotten how little water that baby food required, because what we had was a bowl of mush! I was insistent that if we added more baby food, it would work, so I kept adding more and more. After emptying the box, I tried adding flour. Well, after spending forty-five minutes trying to turn this box of baby cereal into play dough, I ended up with a bowl of very disgusting-looking baby mush. It was pretty icky, and we laughed about it for quite a while as I tried to unstick my fingers. (Maybe it would make a great glue?)

Each recipe in this book contains a suggestion for an activity. Often these suggestions are interchangeable with other recipes, so feel free to explore these activities and to create some of your own as well. Frequently children need only a nudge to get started, and then they will come up with their own ideas. Each activity will have its own unique result and will vary according to the ability and age of the child. This is a great way to introduce children to creativity and art. However, I would also recommend visits to your local art museums, children's museums, and libraries.

When preparing and using the recipes, as when supervising children in any activity, always be informed of the health background of each child under your care. Because mere exposure to an allergen, not only ingestion, can cause a life-threatening allergic reaction, it is essential that you are aware of any allergies a child may have. Common allergens include, but are not limited to, nut products and wheat.

While some older children are able to prepare the recipes, younger children need supervision and guidance. Know how much each child is capable of doing safely. Little ones can help with simple steps like measuring ingredients into a bowl, but they may have problems stirring when certain recipes thicken. Always supervise the concocting and creating, and be on stove duty whenever cooking is required.

I hope this book brings your family, friends, and students much joy and many days of creative fun and learning. It has for mine, and now I no longer have to go to the library to find what I am looking for. I just go to my kitchen counter!

Part 1: Doughs

Helpful Hints for Cooked and Uncooked Doughs

Play doughs are great fun, and you can make many variations to enhance the creative experience. Working with doughs offers hands-on fun while improving your child's fine motor skills and increasing his or her imagination. With young children, start off with simple doughs. As they get older, toss in a few new enhancements. Below you will find ideas for adding color, scent, and texture to doughs, baking and storing them, and other creative, helpful hints.

COLOR AND SCENT

There are many different ways to color the dough. Try using one of the following products to vary the color and aroma: acrylic paint, powdered tempera, unsweetened drink mix, baking cocoa, instant coffee, crushed chalk, baking food color paste, and, of course, food coloring.

TEXTURE

Texture provides a great opportunity for kids to explore the way things feel. Try adding small quantities of the following items for a different look and feel: sand, coffee, wheat germ, glitter, confetti, flower petals, herbal tea grounds, coconut, cornmeal, and spices. You may need to add an extra tablespoon or two of water when adding textures to dough.

LONGER SHELF LIFE

If you take care of your dough by storing it properly, most dough will last anywhere from two to four weeks. I recommend tossing it after one month because of contamination and germs. Always store your doughs in the refrigerator in an airtight plastic container or bag. Simple salt and flour doughs, as well as those containing alum and cream of tartar, can stay on a shelf in a sealed container or bag. You can add one tablespoon of cream of tartar or alum to just about any recipe to keep it fresh longer and to deter molding.

BAKING

If you have colored dough, try glazing it with egg white or evaporated milk for a shinier, browner look. Most dough can be baked to hasten drying time. The safest temperatures for dough are between 200 and 300 degrees. The time varies from one half hour to two hours, depending on the size and thickness of the creation. If a baking temperature is not mentioned on a recipe, test out one creation first at 200 degrees. DO NOT bake sawdust clays. You can also allow dough creations to air dry on a baking sheet for two to three days.

IDEAS

The best part about working with play dough is the varying levels of creativity that can take place. Try adding plastic eyeballs, sequins, or beads with glue. If you are air drying, push accessories or additions into the dough. Paint creations with tempera instead of coloring the dough. Put on a sealant such as shellac, clear nail polish, clear enamel, glaze, or spray. Make ornaments, name plates, animals, or beads. For beads and ornaments, poke holes with straws before baking or air drying, then use a shiny sealant. Have young children use beginner scissors for cutting practice on dough or mold alphabets and numbers. Try pressing flat decorations such as smooth glass, colorful rocks, or marbles into dough for plaques.

COOKED
PLAY DOUGH

BAKING SODA PLAY DOUGH

2 CUPS BAKING SODA
1 CUP CORN STARCH
1 1/4 CUPS COLD WATER
FOOD COLORING IF DESIRED

1. Mix all ingredients in pot.
2. Cook and stir over medium heat until thickened to the consistency of mashed potatoes.
3. Spread out mixture on plate or counter until cool.
4. Once cool, knead for 1–2 minutes.
5. To bake, preheat oven to 200 degrees and bake for about 1 hour.

HINTS: You can paint with shellac, nail polish, or poster paints. The dough can be stored in an airtight container for up to 2 weeks.

SUGGESTIONS: Bailey and I found that this play dough was very pliable, making it great for creating a variety of objects. We made snakes, mountains, and hills. For the older child try baking different sizes of beads. Roll the dough into the desired shape and poke holes with toothpicks. Bake the beads as directed above. Save painting for last. Once the paint has dried, coat with shellac or nail polish.

NOTES:

_____

_____

_____

_____

_____

_____

_____

_____

COCOA DOUGH

1 CUP FLOUR
1/2 CUP SALT
2 TEASPOONS CREAM OF TARTAR
1 TABLESPOON VEGETABLE OIL
1 CUP WATER
2 TABLESPOONS BAKING COCOA

1. Combine all ingredients in a sauce pan. Mix until well blended.
2. Cook over medium heat, stirring occasionally, until mixture forms a ball of dough.
3. Allow to cool for 2 minutes or until mixture is cool enough to handle.
4. Knead on the countertop for 2–3 minutes.
5. Cut and create.

HINTS: Store in an airtight container or Ziploc bag.

SUGGESTIONS: This dough is awesome! It has a great chocolate brown color and smells good. Use for mountains, animals, logs, and other creations. Since this dough is brown, we had fun making a pretend chocolate cake and decorating it with colorful beads and glitter. Older children who need more challenge can try using the dough to etch faces of friends, creating the eyes, ears, nose, etc. Small tools like toothpicks, clay tools (found in craft stores), butter knives, and the ends of paint brushes are great for this project.

NOTES:

_____

_____

_____

_____

_____

_____

_____

COOKED PLAY DOUGH

2 CUPS FLOUR
1 CUP SALT
2 CUPS WATER
4 TABLESPOONS OIL
4 TEASPOONS CREAM OF TARTAR
FOOD COLORING

1. Mix dry ingredients together.
2. Add wet ingredients, including food coloring if desired.
3. Stir in a large sauce pan over medium heat.
4. When mixture pulls away from sides and forms a ball, remove from heat.
5. Turn mixture onto counter and knead 10–15 times.
6. Model.
7. Bake at 250 degrees for 1–3 hours, depending on size of object.

HINTS: Store in airtight container.

SUGGESTIONS: Cooked play dough is one of my favorite recipes because it has so many uses. One fun project is making a name plaque. Cut off a piece of the dough. Roll it into a rectangle about 4 inches by 8–10 inches and set aside. Next, roll out long pieces of dough and form the letters for the names. Place the letters on the square piece of dough and squish the edges into the dough and bake. Younger children may need help with this step. Bake the plaque and letters together, or bake separate and glue the letters onto the plaque. Paint if desired.

NOTES:

_____

_____

_____

_____

CORNSTARCH AND SALT CLAY

2 CUPS SALT
2/3 CUP WATER
1 CUP CORNSTARCH
1/3 CUP WATER

1. Mix salt and 2/3 cup water in a pot.
2. Mix cornstarch and 1/3 cup water in a separate bowl.
3. Stir the salt and water on the stove until it comes to a slow boil.
4. Next, add the cornstarch and water mixture.
5. Remove from stove after it starts to form a dough consistency.
6. Knead on wax paper or freezer paper.
7. Make models with clay and allow several hours for them to dry.
8. Paint when dry.

SUGGESTIONS: For a good spring project try making different things that children see in the spring. Items I found that were great include butterflies, beetles, slugs, snails, caterpillars, and spring flowers.

NOTES:
_____
_____
_____
_____
_____
_____
_____
_____
_____
_____
_____

SAWDUST AND CORNSTARCH CLAY

3 LEVEL TABLESPOONS CORNSTARCH
1 CUP WATER
1 1/2 CUPS OF CLEAN AND DRY SAWDUST

1. In a pot mix cornstarch and water.
2. Cook mixture over medium heat until thickened like pudding.
3. Slowly mix in sawdust, take off burner, and mix well.
4. Turn out onto countertop.
5. Knead until smooth. Add more sawdust, if needed, until you achieve a pliable dough that will not crack apart as you work with it.
6. Mold on wax paper. Let air dry for 1–2 days.

SUGGESTIONS: Try this dough for making trees, logs, and rocks. Push your finger into the middle of trees and logs and put small plastic animals in them. This will give them a lived-in look!

NOTES:

_____

_____

_____

_____

_____

_____

_____

_____

_____

_____

_____

_____

_____

UNCOOKED
PLAY DOUGH

BAKER'S CLAY ORNAMENT DOUGH

4 CUPS FLOUR
1 CUP SALT
1 1/2 CUP WATER
POWDERED TEMPERA PAINT OR FOOD COLORING

1. Mix ingredients with hands in bowl. Add more water if needed.
2. Knead for 5 minutes on a floured board. Add desired coloring during kneading process.
3. Shape dough as desired.
4. Use a straw to make holes in ornaments for hanging.
5. Bake on cookie sheet at 300 degrees for 1/2–1 hour, depending on size and thickness of creation.

SUGGESTIONS: This dough is excellent for ornament making. Also try making letters and baking them for lots of alphabet fun. If you make doubles of letters, use them for sight-word recognition.

NOTES:

BASIC MODELING DOUGH

5 CUPS FLOUR
1 CUP SALT
1/2 CUP VEGETABLE OIL
2 CUPS HOT WATER
FOOD COLORING

1. Combine all ingredients in a bowl and mix well.
2. Turn dough out onto a floured board and knead until smooth.
3. If you like, separate dough into equal portions and add a few drops of food coloring to each portion, thus creating different colored doughs to work with.

HINTS: This recipe is quick and will make at least 4 different colored clumps. Great for a group of 4–5 children. Store in airtight plastic bags and keep refrigerated for longer use.

SUGGESTIONS: Flatten this dough to 1/4 inch thickness. Trace a circle shape with a bowl and cut out. Flatten another piece of dough and have your child lay his or her hand on it. Cut out the hand print with a butter knife. Next ball up a piece of foil about 1 1/2–2 inches thick and place in center of the circle of dough. Lay hand print on top. Press the finger tips into the round dough piece to adhere. Bake in the oven at 200 degrees until hard. After the hand print has cooled, pull out the foil. Have the children push dried flowers in between the fingertips for extra decoration.

NOTES:

_____

_____

_____

_____

_____

_____

_____

BREAD MODELING DOUGH

7–8 PIECES WHITE BREAD
6 DROPS LEMON JUICE OR 1 TEASPOON LIQUID DISH SOAP
6 TABLESPOONS WHITE GLUE

1. Trim crusts from white bread.
2. Break up bread into small pieces and mix with white glue.
3. Mash mixture with the back of a spoon.
4. Add lemon juice or dish soap.
5. Grease hands with vegetable shortening to keep dough from sticking to hands. Knead dough 5–10 minutes or until smooth.
6. Have kids grease hands lightly. Model.
7. Air dry 2–3 days until model dries hard.

HINTS: When the creation is dry you can glaze it with a glaze from a craft store or with clear nail polish. Refrigerate leftovers and use within 1–3 days to prevent mold. Since dough contains glue, rinse dishes quickly and thoroughly.

SUGGESTIONS: Since this dough does not make a large quantity, try this fun project: flatten dough to 1/8 inch thickness. Use a quarter or large button to cut out small circles. Take a toothpick and punch out two button holes in each circle before the dough dries. Continue doing this until you have used up all the dough. After the dough is thoroughly dried, you may decorate your buttons. Use the buttons for stringing practice. Do not use as real buttons, though!

NOTES:
_____
_____
_____
_____
_____

CINNAMON DECORATION DOUGH

1 CUP CINNAMON
3/4 CUP APPLESAUCE
1/4 CUP WHITE GLUE
STRAW

1. In a bowl mix cinnamon, applesauce, and white glue together.
2. Knead dough until smooth.
3. Use cookie cutters to create ornaments. You can use the straw to make holes for hanging.
4. Let the shapes dry for two days, then you can add ribbon or string for hanging.

SUGGESTIONS: Bailey and I used this dough for decorations. We used open-ended cookie cutters because they work better. We also added some gold glitter for sparkling fun.

NOTES:

_____
_____
_____
_____
_____
_____
_____
_____
_____
_____
_____
_____
_____

CORNMEAL DOUGH

1 1/2 CUPS FLOUR
1 1/2 CUPS CORNMEAL
3/4 CUP SALT
1 CUP WATER
1 TABLESPOON OIL

1. Mix all ingredients in a bowl.
2. Add more water if needed to form a smooth dough.
3. Model.
4. Air dry.

HINTS: Store in an airtight bag or container. Keeps up to 1 month if sealed.

SUGGESTIONS: Make this dough into a game! Have each child participating make a flat object. For example; a ball, shapes, alphabets, pear, banana, or toys. When the shapes have dried (you can bake at a low temperature to shorten the process), let the children paint their objects to give them more distinction. Now for the game, lay the clay objects in front of the children and tell them to close their eyes for a moment. Take one of the objects away. Then have the children open their eyes and tell you which one is missing. As they get the hang of it, add more clay objects.

NOTES:

_____
_____
_____
_____
_____
_____
_____
_____
_____

GINGERBREAD PLAY DOUGH

3/4 CUP FLOUR
1/2 CUP SALT
1 1/2 TEASPOONS POWDERED ALUM
1 1/2 TEASPOONS VEGETABLE OIL
1/2 CUP BOILING WATER
BROWN PASTE FOOD COLORING
1 1/2 TEASPOONS PUMPKIN PIE SPICE

1. In a bowl combine the flour, salt, and alum.
2. Add the oil and boiling water.
3. Mix well, then add the spice and food coloring.
4. Knead dough on a floured board until smooth.
5. Use a straw to make holes in ornaments for hanging.
6. Allow to dry one day on one side, then gently turn over and dry on other side for two days.

HINTS: Store in an airtight container or plastic bag until ready to use.

SUGGESTIONS: Look in your local craft store and grocery stores for 3 or 4 different sizes of cookie cutters of gingerbread men. Have children make one of each size to make a gingerbread family.

NOTES:

_____
_____
_____
_____
_____
_____

NO COOK ALUM CLAY

1 CUP FLOUR
1/2 CUP SALT
1/2 CUP + 2–3 TABLESPOONS WARM WATER
1 TEASPOON OF POWDERED ALUM
2 TABLESPOONS VEGETABLE OIL
1 TEASPOON POWDERED TEMPERA PAINT

1. Mix all ingredients together until they form a dough.
2. Knead until smooth.

HINTS: Separate dough into two parts and add tempera or food coloring for two different colors. Add 1 extra tablespoon of water if dough is too crumbly.

SUGGESTIONS: Use this dough to practice cutting skills. Give the children rolling pins and age-appropriate scissors. Ask the children to use the scissors to cut out various shapes like a square and circle. After they master simple shapes, have them cut out more difficult figures like diamonds and stars. Enjoy creating. Use your imagination!

NOTES:

_____
_____
_____
_____
_____
_____
_____
_____
_____
_____
_____

NO COOK PLAY DOUGH

1 1/2 CUPS WHITE FLOUR
1/2 CUP SALT
2 TABLESPOONS OIL
FOOD COLORING
WATER

1. Mix flour, salt, and oil in a bowl.
2. Mix food coloring and water in a separate container.
3. Add colored water to flour mixture until it reaches the consistency of bread dough.

SUGGESTIONS: For a fun project for little ones, purchase a bag of small craft sticks, then tell the children to make balls of clay. Make a sample one about 1/2 inch in diameter. Show them how to push the sticks through the clay and make different structures by adding more clay to each end. Give older children toothpicks. They will need to make smaller balls of clay. Have them try making bridges or geometric shapes. This is a fun challenge!

NOTES:

_____
_____
_____
_____
_____
_____
_____
_____
_____
_____
_____
_____

OAT FLOUR DOUGH

1 3/4 CUPS OAT FLOUR
1/2 TEASPOON ALUM
1/2 CUP SALT
1 TABLESPOON VEGETABLE OIL
3/4 CUP HOT WATER

1. Combine all ingredients in a bowl.

2. Stir until well mixed and forms a ball.

3. Turn out onto an oat-floured board or countertop.

4. Grease hands lightly to avoid dough sticking to hands.

5. Knead small amounts of oat flour into the ball of dough until the dough is no longer overly sticky.

HINTS: This dough has a great texture. It is awesome for kids who are allergic to wheat products. It can be baked at 200 degrees for 1/2–1 hour, depending on the size and thickness of the creation. Store in an airtight bag or container. Refrigerate for longer play life.

SUGGESTIONS: To help children learn colors, have them make two flat pieces of play dough any shape they like, around 3 x 3 inches. After they have finished, bake their creations. When they have cooled, give the children their two shapes back. (Remember, they don't have to match.) Give each child one color of tempera paint—be sure to give each child a different color. Have them paint one side of their shapes, leaving the other side plain. Allow the paint to dry. When this is done mix all the shapes up and turn painted side down. Now they can play the memory game with their colors!

NOTES:

_____

_____

_____

_____

_____

OATMEAL PLAY DOUGH

1 CUP QUICK OATMEAL
1/2 CUP WATER
1/2 CUP FLOUR
1/4 CUP SALT
FOOD COLORING

1. Blend oatmeal in a blender until slightly finer for a smoother textured dough.
2. Combine remaining ingredients with oatmeal in a bowl.
3. Stir mixture until smooth.
4. Grease hands with shortening and knead dough for 2–3 minutes on a well-floured countertop.
5. Add food coloring if desired during kneading.

HINTS: This dough has a nice grainy natural texture, not too sticky. Store in refrigerator for another day.

SUGGESTIONS: Allow the children to create objects on their own. Give them beads or buttons to decorate their creations. Tell them to use their imaginations to create a new type of flower, animal, or bug. As the children finish their original creations, ask them to tell you a story about it. Write down each child's story on lined paper, leaving room for pictures. Set up a separate table with crayons so that the children who are finished can illustrate their stories while you finish up with the other children. After they have finished their stories, staple each one. Allow the creations to dry. Now they have a story and a new creation!

NOTES:
_____
_____
_____
_____
_____

PLAIN MODELING DOUGH

4 1/2 CUPS FLOUR
3/4 CUP SALT
1/4 CUP LIQUID JOY DISH SOAP
1 3/4 CUPS WATER
FOOD COLORING

1. Combine all ingredients in a bowl and mix well.
2. Turn out onto a floured board and knead until smooth. Add more flour if too sticky.

HINTS: Separate into sections and create different colors by adding a few drops of food coloring to each clump. Store in airtight plastic bags and keep refrigerated for longer use.

SUGGESTIONS: This project is a lot of fun for learning left and right. With a rolling pin have your children flatten the dough to 1/4 inch thickness on wax paper. Next, have them take off their shoes and socks. Put the wax paper and dough on the floor and let them step on the dough. Using a plastic butter knife, trace the shapes of their feet. After that step is done, move the dough back to the table. Trim off the excess dough and, using a pencil, write Left and Right on the correct footprint. Allow the footprints to dry thoroughly.

NOTES:
_____
_____
_____
_____
_____
_____
_____
_____
_____
_____

SAWDUST AND FLOUR CLAY

1 CUP FLOUR
2 CUPS CLEAN DRY SAWDUST
2 TABLESPOONS SALT
1 CUP WATER

1. Mix flour, sawdust, and salt.
2. Add water until the dough is thick and pliable. Actual amount of water may vary depending on whether the sawdust is fine or course.

HINTS: Makes a nice dough for molding.

SUGGESTIONS: Have children shape this dough into the shape of an egg. Ask them to gently cut the egg open but not all the way through. (Both halves should be still attached.) Next, give them artificial baby chicks (found in craft stores in the spring time) to place in the middle of the eggs. Reshape egg if the egg starts to lose its shape when being cut in half. Allow to dry.

NOTES:

_____

_____

_____

_____

_____

_____

_____

_____

_____

_____

_____

_____

SENSORY DOUGH

5 CUPS FLOUR
1 CUP SALT
1/2 CUP VEGETABLE OIL
2 CUPS HOT WATER
SENSORY ITEMS:
unsweetened drink mix, glitter, sand, paper, vermiculite,
coffee grounds, cornmeal, flower petals,
food coloring, sawdust, or your choice

1. Mix flour, salt, vegetable oil, and water together.
2. Knead dough until smooth.
3. Divide dough into 4—6 balls or clumps.
4. Mix a different sensory item into each clump or ball.

HINTS: This is great for a group of children.

SUGGESTIONS: Use this dough according to the sensory item you placed in the dough. For example, when you use sand, ask the child to create a miniature sand castle or beach scene. If you use glitter, ask them to create planets and stars. For scents, ask them to create fruits like lemons and grapes. With flower petals, have them make different flowers like roses and daisies. Let the play begin!

NOTES: _____

_____

_____

_____

_____

_____

_____

_____

SPARKLING PAPER MOLDING MIX

2 CUPS CONSTRUCTION PAPER SCRAPS
(one color or like colors)
4 1/2 CUPS WATER
1/2–3/4 CUP FLOUR
1–2 TABLESPOONS GLITTER

1. Tear paper into small pieces.

2. Place paper and 4 cups of water into a blender. Let soak 2–3 minutes, then blend until mixture turns into pulp.

3. Squeeze excess water from pulp and put it in a bowl. Measure out desired amount of glitter and pour on top of pulp.

4. Mix flour and remaining water with the paper pulp until blended. Start with a 1/2 cup of flour, working up to 3/4 cup as needed, depending on the remaining water content of the pulp.

5. Knead until a dough forms. Mixture will be sticky and may seem wrong, but it is fine. Don't worry.

6. Have kids smear a small amount of shortening on their hands. Spread wax paper on table. Push mixture into double open-sided cookie cutters, then gently push out onto wax paper, or mold mix into figures.

7. Finished creations should air dry in a day or two. Rotate every six hours or so for better drying results.

HINTS: You can also take out the glitter and try adding confetti, beads, or dried flowers for another unique look! It's very sticky but creates fun results. Try using on a floured board. Spray cookie cutters that are open only on one side with nonstick cooking spray. You can spray with a clear varnish for a protective coating.

SUGGESTIONS: Kids can make all kinds of creations with this sparkling molding mix. They can make free form sculpture, gift tags, and ornaments. For best results, use a light colored paper. Flatten the dough on wax paper. Allow the dough to air dry for a full day. After a day it will start to harden on the outside. Adults use scissors to cut into the dough and cut out desired shapes. Poke holes with a straw. Turn on other side and continue drying until hard.

NOTES:

_____

_____

_____

_____

_____

_____

_____

_____

_____

_____

_____

_____

_____

_____

_____

_____

_____

_____

_____

_____

_____

STRETCHY DOUGH

1/4 CUP WHITE GLUE
1/2 CUP FLOUR
1/2 CUP CORNSTARCH
1/4 CUP WATER
FOOD COLORING

1. Mix glue, water, and food coloring in bowl. Stir until blended.

2. Mix flour and cornstarch in another bowl.

3. Slowly mix the two mixtures together until a stiff dough is formed.

4. Knead for 2–3 minutes or until smooth on floured wax paper (for easier cleanup).

5. Mold on a covered surface such as wax paper or the shiny side of freezer paper.

6. Drying time depends on the size of your art.

HINTS: It's a pliable, stretchy dough with a smooth texture. Not good with cookie cutters because it sticks to the paper. Molding the dough is more successful.

SUGGESTIONS: Ask children to mold the dough into a cookie shape. They can decorate their "cookie" however they like, using an assortment of colored beads, confetti, or pieces of brown paper and a hole puncher. Explain to them that just as there are no two cookies exactly alike, no two children are alike. They are all special just the way they are!!

NOTES:

_____

_____

_____

_____

_____

_____

_____

EDIBLE
PLAY DOUGH

HELPFUL HINTS FOR EDIBLE DOUGHS

Edible play doughs are great for toddlers! They offer fun for little ones who explore with their mouths as well as their hands. Just follow these great tips for additional ideas.

BEFORE YOU BEGIN

Edible play doughs are a lot of fun, but you want to make sure you have cleaned all surfaces well to eliminate the possibility of germs. Then lay down wax paper or freezer paper (shiny side up) for the children to play on. Be sure the little ones have clean hands and faces. Move all other objects, except those to be played with, from the table to avoid spills or mishaps.

MAKING THE DOUGH

I don't recommend the candy modeling clay for toddlers, because it contains too much sugar. Make sure that it is safe for your young child to eat honey. You can check with your pediatrician or omit it from the recipe. Do not use recipes containing peanut butter if your child is allergic to peanuts. When adding food coloring, remember that just a few drops will do. Use only clean utensils, bowls, and surfaces for making the dough. If you are making a large batch and are only using a little at a time, be sure that you store the unused portion in an airtight plastic bag in the refrigerator. Give children only the amount of dough that they will actually play with. Doing this will eliminate waste and save some fun for another day.

AFTER PLAYTIME

After playtime is finished, simply throw the used dough away. For easier cleanup roll wax paper with used dough into a ball and throw in the trash. Wipe up any spills on floor to avoid slipping. Remove and clean playtime utensils.

CANDY MODELING CLAY

1 POUND POWDERED SUGAR
1/2 TEASPOON SALT
1/3 CUP CORN SYRUP
1/3 CUP SOFTENED MARGARINE
1 TEASPOON VANILLA
FOOD COLORING (OPTIONAL)

1. Mix all ingredients except food coloring together in a bowl.
2. Stir until well blended by pushing margarine into sugar gradually. Push mix together with hands to begin forming a ball of dough.
3. Add more powdered sugar if needed.
4. Turn out onto wax paper and knead for 2 minutes.
5. Break into clumps or balls and add food coloring if desired.
6. Sculpt.
7. Air dry to harden.

HINTS: Add different flavorings like banana, mint, or almond. Because candy modeling clay is mostly sugar, I don't recommend it for toddlers. I recommend giving each child a portion the size of a golf ball to start with. Store unused portion in refrigerator.

SUGGESTIONS: This clay is great for different edible animals, decorations, fruits, or plants. Decorate with sugar sprinkles and candy. Kids can eat their edible treat or use them to top cupcakes.

NOTES:
_____
_____
_____
_____
_____
_____

INSTANT POTATO DOUGH

1 CUP BOILING WATER
1 1/2 CUPS INSTANT MASHED POTATOES
FOOD COLORING (OPTIONAL)

1. Put instant potatoes in a bowl.
2. Pour boiling water on top and stir well. Add food coloring if desired.
3. Pour mixture out onto wax paper and knead until it forms an easy-to-work-with dough.
4. Add more instant potatoes if needed.

HINTS: This is a great edible dough for little ones. Just make sure all working surfaces are very clean and all hands have been washed!

SUGGESTIONS: Toddlers and preschoolers are beginning to develop their fine motor skills. As they gain more control, have them begin to make shapes out of the dough. For instance, show them how to roll the dough into a ball shape or into a box-shaped present.

NOTES:

_____

_____

_____

_____

_____

_____

_____

_____

_____

_____

_____

_____

_____

OATMEAL DOUGH

1/2 CUP FLOUR
1/2 CUP WATER
1 CUP QUICK COOKING OATMEAL

1. Combine all ingredients in a bowl.
2. Mix well.
3. Turn out onto a floured countertop.
4. Knead dough for 2–3 minutes.

HINTS: Add food coloring if you like. Store in an airtight container.

SUGGESTIONS: This dough is great for beginners. Toddlers can explore away, and you can feel comfortable letting them do so. Young children often need to be shown how to manipulate play dough. Set out a rolling pin and cookie cutters. Show children how to flatten dough either with their hands or with the rolling pin. Take the cookie cutter and press into the dough. Have the children imitate what you do. Show them how to roll the dough out into a snake shape also.

NOTES:

OATMEAL PLAY DOUGH

2 CUPS FLOUR
4 CUPS OATMEAL
1 CUP WATER
1 CUP WHITE CORN SYRUP
1 CUP PEANUT BUTTER
1 1/4 CUPS NONFAT POWDERED MILK
1 1/4 CUPS SIFTED POWDERED SUGAR

1. Combine flour and oatmeal in a blender and grind together for 30 seconds.
2. Empty flour and oatmeal into bowl and add 1 cup water and knead.
3. Add corn syrup, peanut butter, nonfat powdered milk, and powdered sugar.
4. Combine and knead well. If mixture is too sticky, add extra flour with a tablespoon.
5. Separate into balls of 3 inches or so. Give each child a ball of dough.
6. Put out bowls of chocolate or butterscotch chips, sunflower seeds, raisins, shelled peanuts, and banana chips for children to decorate their creations with.
7. Let children eat their creations!

HINTS: Can be stored in refrigerator in airtight plastic bags. Keeps well.

SUGGESTIONS: Kids can turn their edible dough into an extra fun treat. If you put out sunflower seeds, ask the children to make a sunflower, using the dough as the base and the seeds to fill it as you would with a mosaic. Use banana chips for making a banana, chocolate chips to make a model of a chocolate kiss.

NOTES:

_____

_____

_____

_____

_____

PEANUT BUTTER CLAY DOUGH

1 18 OUNCE JAR OF CREAMY PEANUT BUTTER
1/2 CUP HONEY
2 CUPS INSTANT NONFAT POWDERED MILK
1/2 CUP CHOCOLATE CHIPS (OPTIONAL)
WAX PAPER

1. Combine peanut butter and honey in mixing bowl.
2. Add instant powdered milk, 1/2 cup at a time until mixture forms a dough.
3. Have children cover hands with powdered sugar or powdered milk so the dough doesn't stick to their hands.
4. Allow children to make shapes, small critters, letters, or numbers. Decorate with chocolate chips.
5. Eat!

HINTS: Use within 1–2 days.

SUGGESTIONS: This dough can be made into a great project for children who are learning to read. Ask the kids to shape the dough to look like letters. Have them practice putting the letters into simple words, or even their own name. They can eat the letters once they have correctly spelled and sounded the word.

NOTES:

_____

_____

_____

_____

_____

_____

_____

_____

PEANUT BUTTER AND WHEAT GERM DOUGH

3 TABLESPOONS PEANUT BUTTER
3 TABLESPOONS TOASTED WHEAT GERM
1 TABLESPOON HONEY
1 TABLESPOON POWDERED MILK

1. Mix all ingredients in a small bowl.
2. Knead with a small amount of powdered milk.
3. Let your child mold away.

HINTS: Add small edible goodies like M&Ms, chocolate chips, coconut, Skittles, raisins, etc. to creation, if desired. Refrigerate your child's creation before eating as a nice cold snack! Use within 1–2 days. This dough tends to dry out after a couple of days in the refrigerator. Recipe is enough for one child to have fun. May double or triple recipe to accommodate more children.

SUGGESTIONS: Ask children to model their favorite kind of candy out of this dough. Maybe a lollipop, candy cane, or bubble gum. Give them sprinkles and colored sugar to make it look more like a candy. Have them tell you about their candy.

NOTES:
_____
_____
_____
_____
_____
_____
_____
_____

SIMPLE PEANUTTY PLAY CLAY

1 CUP PEANUT BUTTER
1 CUP + 1 TABLESPOON POWDERED MILK
1 TABLESPOON HONEY (OPTIONAL)

1. Add all ingredients together in a bowl and mix well.
2. Add more powdered milk if it is still too sticky or not stiff enough.
3. Roll, cut out with cookie cutters, and decorate with raisins, chocolate chips, licorice, coconut, M&Ms, Skittles, marshmallows, or your child's favorite snack.
4. Chill snack, if desired.

HINTS: This recipe is good for a group of 4–5 toddlers or preschool-age children. Each child will have enough dough to make a creation for snack time! Kid tasted; kid approved! Break off a few pieces at a time for kids to work with and store remainder in the refrigerator for the next day. It should be used within 1–2 days, or it will dry out. Toss all leftovers from work/play area.

SUGGESTIONS: While doing letter reviews with children, make it fun by giving them this dough. Set out flash cards of the letters you are reviewing. Ask the kids to shape the dough like the letters. When they are finished, go over the sounds the dough letters make before eating them!

NOTES:

_____

_____

_____

_____

_____

_____

_____

_____

_____

LANDSCAPE AND RELIEF MAP DOUGH

BLUE WATER DOUGH FOR MAPS

1 CUP SALT
1 CUP FLOUR
2/3 CUP WATER
BLUE FOOD COLORING

1. Mix salt and flour together in a bowl.
2. Slowly add water a little at a time until mixture resembles thick frosting.
3. Add blue food coloring to achieve desired color.
4. Use a small spoon or craft stick to drizzle or smear mixture in the desired areas.
5. Allow to dry for a day or two.

SUGGESTIONS: This dough is great as an accessory to a map-making project for school! Have your child draw a map, real or imaginary, on a piece of cardboard. Use the dough to fill in waterfalls, rivers, lakes, and oceans. You can also make a 3-D ocean. Here's how: use the relief map dough (p. 56, add more flour to thicken enough to shape) to create the bottom of the ocean floor in the bottom of a large shoe box, forming star fish, a coral reef, small tropical fish, anemones, sea fans, and tube sponges. After you have made the living creatures, fill in around them with the blue water dough. Allow 3–4 days to dry. Paint carefully if desired. For the last step, place blue-colored plastic wrap over the top. Tape the plastic around the edges of the box. Now you can look into your 3-D ocean. This is a great way to research ocean floor life.

NOTES:

_____

_____

_____

_____

_____

_____

_____

COFFEE RELIEF MAP DOUGH

1 CUP COFFEE GROUNDS
1 CUP FLOUR
1 CUP SALT
1 CUP WATER

1. Mix all ingredients in a bowl and stir until well blended. If the dough is too runny, add a little more flour one tablespoon at a time.
2. Use a large craft stick to apply mixture to cardboard map.
3. Let mixture dry overnight.

HINTS: This works great on maps for mountain sculpting. To make snowy alps, try applying powdered sugar or flour to mountain tops, or after the mixture has dried, apply puffed-up snow paint (p. 70) to the peaks.

SUGGESTIONS: Children can look through a book on our solar system to see what planets look like, and then create the surface of one of these planets out of the dough. Use other map-making doughs to produce different looks. Explore the various textures of the doughs.

NOTES:

_____
_____
_____
_____
_____
_____
_____
_____
_____
_____
_____

FLAT PLAINS MAP DOUGH

1 CUP SALT
1/2 CUP FLOUR
1/2 CUP WATER
1 TEASPOON BAKING COCOA OR BROWN FOOD PASTE

1. Mix all ingredients in a bowl and stir until blended.
2. Spread mixture with butter knife, spoon, or large craft stick onto cardboard map.
3. To build up small hills or valleys allow first coat to dry, then build up to desired height. Dry for 2–3 days before painting.

HINTS: This dough will dry hard and keep indefinitely. Try pushing fingers through dough to make indents for rivers or lakes, then fill with blue water dough (p. 53). If desired, paint when completely dry. Coat with clear craft spray or shellac for a shiny look.

SUGGESTIONS: Have children create a desert scene with this dough. Research the desert together and see what animals and vegetation live there. Supply the children with miniatures of cacti and other desert items, or give them play dough to create their own cacti. Help the children bring the desert scene to life with desert animals such as camels. You can try constructing other regions as well.

NOTES:

_____

_____

_____

_____

_____

_____

_____

_____

_____

_____

RELIEF MAP DOUGH

1 CUP SALT
3/4 CUP FLOUR
1/2 CUP WARM WATER

1. Mix all ingredients in a bowl until blended.
2. Turn out onto cardboard map and use fingers or large craft stick to push around as needed.
3. Allow to dry for 2–4 days.

HINTS: Add miniature flags, trees, and other items while dough is still soft to ensure items will be held in place. Dough will dry hard, and because it is thick, it does not require building up. Paint, if desired, after dough has thoroughly dried.

SUGGESTIONS: Use this dough for large mountains, volcanoes, or entire countries. A fun creative art project is to create a fantasy future world. Kids get creative by constructing new architecture, roads, and forms of transportation. What will the world look like years from now? Why not ask the future generation what they think?

NOTES:

_____
_____
_____
_____
_____
_____
_____
_____
_____
_____
_____
_____

VOLCANO AND LANDSCAPE DOUGH

1 CUP COFFEE GROUNDS (UNUSED)
1 1/8 CUP FLOUR
1 CUP SALT
1 CUP WATER

1. Mix all ingredients into a bowl.
2. Stir until well blended.
3. Turn out mixture onto a floured board. Knead dough for 2–3 minutes.
4. Bake dough in oven at 200 degrees for 1 hour or air dry on a cookie rack.

HINTS: Landscape dough makes great rocks, trees, logs, and other nature items. Make a double batch of this dough and turn out onto cardboard for an awesome volcano. Mound up dough to make a volcano shape. To see an eruption use the lava recipe (p.58).

SUGGESTIONS: Besides the standard volcano and mountains, you can also use this dough to create a beach scene. The coffee grains help it look more like sand. You can lessen the amount of coffee by 1/4 cup and add 1/4 cup sand if desired. Omit 1/8 cup flour so that the dough spreads more easily. After you have created the beach scene, add your beach creatures: sea turtles, crabs, clams, rocks with mussels attached, seagulls, puffins. The seashore has some amazing animals to learn about. Research it by taking a walk on the beach and reading books together. Kids can create their sea life with the basic cooked play dough recipe (p. 19), paint them, and then insert them into the beach scene. Allow project a few days to dry.

NOTES:

_____
_____
_____
_____
_____
_____

LAVA RECIPE FOR VOLCANOES

1/4 CUP BAKING SODA
1/2 CUP WATER
1/2 CUP VINEGAR
1/4 CUP DISHWASHING LIQUID
1 EMPTY CAN WITH ONE END REMOVED
PITCHER
RED FOOD COLORING

1. Press can into the top of the volcano. Leaving the top uncovered, build up dough around the can until it is hidden.
2. Place the baking soda in the can.
3. Mix water, vinegar, dishwashing liquid, and food coloring in the pitcher.
4. Ready for the eruption? Pour the vinegar mixture into the can and watch the "lava" flow!

SUGGESTIONS: Try using various sizes of cans or jars to see how the lava comes out differently. Does the lava come out slower in a small jar or faster? Great for experimenting. Use a timer for accuracy if desired.

NOTES:

_____
_____
_____
_____
_____
_____
_____
_____
_____
_____

Part 2: Paints

HELPFUL HINTS FOR PAINT

Painting offers many learning opportunities. You can allow free-draw art or give the children specific ideas such as people, scenery, fruits and vegetables, flower arrangements, toys, or geometric shapes.

BEGINNING ARTIST: ONE TO THREE YEARS

Instead of buying expensive finger-paint paper, use freezer paper purchased at the local grocery store. For finger painting try using food handler gloves or latex gloves for easy cleaning. Most finger paints will dry overnight. If using brushes, change water frequently. For those just learning to paint, use large kid paint brushes. Set out different shapes of sponges for print art or use household items, like strawberry trays. Set out only one or two colors to start with. Most of all, just allow the children to freely explore.

BUDDING ARTIST: FOUR TO SIX YEARS

It is time to graduate to poster board or thicker paper. Larger, heavier paper allows more freedom. At this stage children are able to draw some shapes and stick people. They also understand about cleaning their brushes after each color. They are beginning to transpose mental images to paper. Don't get me wrong, continue to break out the freezer paper for plain old messy fun, but let's give them tools to see what their imaginations can do. Ask them to paint pictures and describe them to you when they are finished. Ask them about the colors they used. Try having them paint a box-shaped present or a picture of their family. Print or sponge painting is great for wrapping paper and cards. Cut a file folder into one inch by five inch strips, have the artist paint a design on it, let it dry, and then laminate for a book marker. At this age, projects are great but continue to allow for plenty of free exploration time.

THE YOUNG ARTIST AT WORK: SEVEN TO TEN YEARS

I recommend getting into more details at this age. Try a combination of free art and project art. Free art is whatever the child wants to paint, and project art is a specific idea to create or work from. Show children paintings from famous or local artists by going to museums and galleries and checking out books from the library. Try portrait, landscape, primitive, and geometric art. Have kids explore with texture paints, homemade oil paint, and egg paint. Give them thick watercolor paper or poster board. Begin to offer different brushes and sponges (found in craft stores) for painting a variety of forms such as clouds, skies, and trees. Acrylic paints are good starter professional paints and can be thinned and cleaned up with water.

TIPS ON PAINTING

If paint becomes too thick, dilute with water. If paintbrushes are not readily available, use pieces of sponges, cotton swabs, or even cotton balls. If you are painting plastics, mix powdered tempera with liquid dishwashing detergent instead of with water and starch for better adherence. If painting unfinished wood, give it a light coat of shellac or wood sealer so the paint will not soak in. Tempera and poster paints have a dull finish and will not resist moisture, therefore, for protection and shine, spray finished product with clear craft spray or coat with diluted white glue. Clear nail polish works well for small projects. Allow artwork to dry thoroughly before hanging up so the paint does not run.

BRUSH PAINT

ADHESIVE PAINT

2 TABLESPOONS LIQUID TEMPERA PAINT
1 TABLESPOON WHITE GLUE
GLITTER, CONFETTI, COLORED SAND, ETC.

1. Mix the tempera paint and glue.
2. Use the paint mixture for print making (such as potato prints or stamps) or paint a design.
3. Add the glitter or confetti or other items to the paint to give it a unique twist. The glue will help keep the glitter adhered to the paint.

HINTS: This recipe can be doubled.

SUGGESTIONS: Help children cut out an egg shape from a piece of poster board. Have them draw designs on the egg with a pencil and then paint one section at a time. While the paint is still wet, they can further decorate each section with glitter or confetti. With a little creativity, they can make each section look different.

NOTES:
_____
_____
_____
_____
_____
_____
_____
_____
_____
_____
_____

CLOUD PAINT

3–5 DROPS FOOD COLORING
1 TEASPOON WATER

1. Mix food coloring and water. You can make several colors if you like.
2. Paint mixture on white paper to create a cloud-like appearance.

SUGGESTIONS: If you've ever wanted to paint pictures like clouds, here's how! On a nice day with lots of clouds take your paper and paint outside. Let the kids lie down on the grass and stare up at the sky. Point out how certain clouds look like different shapes, faces, or even animals. Let them paint whatever shapes or objects they see in the clouds.

NOTES:

_____
_____
_____
_____
_____
_____
_____
_____
_____
_____
_____
_____
_____
_____
_____

HOMEMADE OIL PAINT

2 TABLESPOONS LIQUID DISH SOAP
2 TABLESPOONS POWDERED TEMPERA PAINT
1/2 TEASPOON WATER

1. Combine all ingredients into a small container until completely blended.
2. Repeat process until you have all the colors desired.
3. Let the paint sit uncovered overnight to thicken for a better canvas paint and to get rid of soap bubbles.

HINTS: This paint can be stored for up to 2 months in airtight containers.

SUGGESTIONS: Research famous artists who used oil paints. Show the children pictures that these artists painted and discuss the techniques they used. Ask the children to paint landscape pictures or portrait art using some of those techniques.

NOTES:

_____

_____

_____

_____

_____

_____

_____

_____

_____

_____

_____

_____

_____

_____

HOMEMADE POSTER PAINT

1/2 CUP CORNSTARCH
3/4 CUP COLD WATER
2 CUPS HOT WATER
1/2 CUP POWDERED DETERGENT
FOOD COLORING OR POWDERED TEMPERA
JARS

1. Combine 1/2 cup cornstarch with the 3/4 cup of cold water in a bowl.
2. Pour cornstarch mixture into a pot and set on stove. Turn burner to medium and add two cups hot water. Cook until mixture boils clear, but NOT thick.
3. Remove from heat and add 1/2 cup of powdered detergent.
4. Stir until blended.
5. Divide mixture into jars.
6. Add a different color of food coloring or powdered tempera paint to each jar.

SUGGESTIONS: A fun project using homemade poster paint is to have the children team up and pretend they are advertising agents promoting a product. They can use a product they already have at home such as cereals, candy, cookies, or chips. Or they can have fun making up their own product. Have them "promote" the product by painting advertising signs. Kids have a great time using their imaginations on this one, plus they get to explore a career.

NOTES:

_____

_____

_____

_____

_____

_____

MILKY PAINT

1/2 CUP POWDERED MILK
3/4 CUP WATER
FOOD COLORING

1. In a bowl, mix powdered milk and water with a whisk until well blended.
2. Divide mixture into 3–5 containers, depending on how many colors you would like to make.
3. Add food coloring to each container and stir until blended.
4. Use paintbrushes for painting on paper.

HINTS: This is a great, easy paint that dries quickly. Have fun!

SUGGESTIONS: Ask the children to paint pictures of their houses. They can paint the outside with the yard or paint a room of their choice, such as the living room, kitchen, dining room, or their bedroom. When finished, ask them to tell you about their house painting and what their favorite place is in their home.

NOTES:

_____

_____

_____

_____

_____

_____

_____

_____

_____

_____

_____

EGG PAINT

BRIGHT COLORED PASTEL CHALKS
1 EGG YOLK
2 TEASPOONS WATER
MUFFIN TIN
PLASTIC BAGS
METAL KITCHEN MALLET

1. Break off small pieces of colored chalk. Separate colors into plastic bags. Pound with side of mallet until powdery.
2. Put a different color of ground chalk into each cup of the muffin tin.
3. In another bowl beat egg yolk and water.
4. Add spoonfuls of egg mixture to the powdered chalk and stir. This will make a nice smooth paint.

HINTS: You can use this recipe and experiment with different ingredients such as crushed berries, mud, crushed flowers, ketchup, crushed charcoal mixed with egg, and fine spices like paprika or cinnamon.

SUGGESTIONS: This is a great paint for creating all kinds of paintings. You can even give your paper an aged look by dragging a wet tea bag across it. Allow the paper to dry before painting your picture.

NOTES:

_____

_____

_____

_____

_____

_____

_____

_____

PUFFED UP SNOW PAINT

1/2 CUP WHITE GLUE
1 CUP SHAVING CREAM

1. Mix glue and shaving cream in a small bowl.
2. Stir the mixture well and allow to rest for 1 minute.
3. Paint onto paper with paintbrushes.

HINTS: This paint is a lot of fun, but it takes time to dry thoroughly. The top layer dries quickly, but the bottom layer takes longer. Allow to dry 24 hours for best results.

SUGGESTIONS: We enjoyed this paint for a number of winter projects. It's great for coating foam balls and making snowmen or snowballs. For awesome snowflakes, cut snowflakes out of thick construction paper and paint them with puff paint. Add glitter for a sparkly look. Since the paint is white, it looks great on blue construction paper. We painted a puffy snowman. After he dried for a day, we painted a face and a hat on him. The paint feels foamy after it dries, and the kids think it's cool.

NOTES:

_____

_____

_____

_____

_____

_____

_____

_____

_____

_____

_____

ROCK PAINT

1 TABLESPOON LIQUID STARCH
1 TABLESPOON POWERED TEMPERA PAINT
ROCKS TO PAINT ON

1. Pick out larger rocks for younger children for better handling. Smaller rocks for older children will be more challenging. Make sure rocks are clean.
2. Mix liquid starch with tempera paint until it is a little thicker than poster paint. Stir with a paintbrush.
3. Repeat recipe to make several different colors.

HINTS: Allow base coat to dry before adding additional colors so that they do not mix.

SUGGESTIONS: Allow the children to be creative. Tell them to use their imaginations and use the rocks to make faces, flowers, animals, snakes, lizards, butterflies, turtles, frogs, or even space rocks. They can glue smaller-sized rocks together, or they can show you how they want them, and you can put them together for them with super glue (hot glue guns work also). After the glue has dried, let the children paint their creations. Add glitter, wiggle eyes, and small pieces of pipe cleaners for legs if desired. When finished, coat each project with clear nail polish or craft spray.

NOTES:

_____

_____

_____

_____

_____

_____

_____

_____

_____

_____

SCRATCH AND SNIFF PAINT

UNSWEETENED DRINK MIX
WATER
SEVERAL SMALL CONTAINERS OR PLASTIC EGG CARTON

1. Mix small amounts of drink mix and water in container or egg carton.
2. Stir until the drink mix has dissolved and the mixture is of a good consistency for painting.
3. Repeat this step as many times as you like to create other colors (and scents) by using different varieties of drink mix.
4. Paint as desired. Allow to dry overnight before scratching and sniffing.

SUGGESTIONS: This paint is great for making scratch and sniff stickers. Here's how: draw pictures of various fruits such as grapes, cherries, and oranges. Then paint the pictures with the appropriate color of scratch and sniff paint. Allow the paint to dry and then cut out the pictures. To make the pictures into stickers, coat the backs with sticker gelatin glue (p. 123) or with a glue stick.

NOTES:

TEXTURE PAINTS

LIQUID TEMPERA PAINT IN VARIOUS COLORS
TEXTURE MATERIALS:
white flour, crushed egg shells, glitter, corn meal,
grits, wheat germ, sawdust, coconut, sand,
confetti, salt, herbal tea grounds,
sequins, various herbs
JARS FOR MIXING
BRUSHES OR CRAFT STICKS
HEAVY PAPER OR POSTER BOARD

1. Fill each jar with 1/8 cup of liquid tempera paint (each a different color).
2. Add one texture material to each jar. For instance: in the first jar add crushed egg shells, in the second color add flour, etc.
3. Each material will present a different texture.
4. Use craft sticks or different paintbrushes to apply texture paint.
5. Dry for several hours.

SUGGESTIONS: Give children an idea to paint from. Here are some possibilities: waterfalls, mountains, ocean life, ancient times, transportation, architecture, weather, nature, flowers, and animals. Using the texture paints, children can create a picture from the idea presented.

NOTES:
_____
_____
_____
_____
_____
_____
_____

FINGER PAINT

BRIGHT GLOSS PAINT

1/4 CUP SWEETENED CONDENSED MILK
1 TABLESPOON LIQUID TEMPERA PAINT
OR 1 PACKET UNSWEETENED DRINK MIX

1. Mix condensed milk and paint in a plastic bowl.
2. Stir until blended.
3. Repeat steps as often as desired to create additional colors.
4. Dry artwork overnight.

HINTS: This paint does not store well for future use unless made the night before and stored in the refrigerator. Use with fingers or a brush. Food coloring or powdered tempera work in a pinch, but the best colors come from unsweetened drink mix and liquid tempera. This is a fun sticky finger paint. Dries shiny. Use the non-shiny side of freezer paper for the best results.

SUGGESTIONS: Here is an easy idea for little children. Ask them to paint a picture of something shiny, like a wrapped present or an apple. Set out something for them to look at. Studying objects is a great way for young children to learn to put down on paper what they see. Always start with simple items, though.

NOTES:

_____
_____
_____
_____
_____
_____
_____
_____
_____
_____

COOKED CORNSTARCH PAINT

1/4 CUP CORNSTARCH
3/4 CUP WATER
3 DIFFERENT COLORS OF FOOD COLORING
OR 1–2 TEASPOONS POWDERED TEMPERA PAINTS
PAPER CUPS

1. Mix cornstarch and water in cooking pot.
2. Stir mixture over low heat. Don't let it stick to the pot.
3. Simmer until creamy white and thick.
4. Divide mixture into paper cups and add food coloring or powdered tempera paints.
5. Stir colors until blended. Allow to cool.
6. Spoon globs onto paper and push colors around with fingers.

HINTS: The consistency of this paint makes it great for no mess painting (p. 85).

SUGGESTIONS: Set out a sheet of paper for each child. Pick two primary colors that will create a secondary color. For example, yellow and blue make green. Spoon a glob of each color onto each sheet of paper. Discuss the colors on the children's papers while they paint. Ask them what is happening to their colors as they mix them together. As well as learning colors, they will learn cause and effect: If I do this to the paint, then this will happen. Kids think it's fun, and it's nice that they still end up with a cool color!

NOTES:

_____
_____
_____
_____
_____
_____
_____

COOKED FINGER PAINT

1 CUP FLOUR
2 TABLESPOONS SALT
2 1/2 CUPS WATER
FOOD COLORING

1. Combine flour, salt, and water in a pot.
2. Mix with a wire whisk until smooth.
3. Continue stirring until mixture boils and starts to thicken.
4. Remove from heat and separate into bowls.
5. Add food coloring in each container.

HINTS: Does not store well.

SUGGESTIONS: Have children paint a piece of thick paper any way they like. They can paint shapes, designs, or a picture. After the pictures have dried, write the children's names across their painting in permanent black marker (avoid covering the actual picture if they did one). Lay each picture on top of a piece of colored construction paper and paste it on. Make sure that the colored paper frames each painting. After the glue has dried, take the pictures to a printing shop to have them laminated. They make great place mats for meal-time or for desktops.

NOTES:

_____

_____

_____

_____

_____

_____

_____

_____

_____

FINGER PAINT FOR BATH TIME

1/3 CUP LIQUID BABY SOAP
1 1/2 TABLESPOONS CORNSTARCH
FOOD COLORING

1. Mix liquid baby soap and cornstarch until well blended.
2. Pour small amounts into different sections of a plastic container such as an egg carton or ice cube tray.
3. Add different colors to each one and mix with a small spoon.

SUGGESTIONS: For bathtime fun, show your child how to paint numbers or letters on the bathtub wall. This is one time they won't get in trouble for writing on the walls! Washes off easily. Let your child have a great time!

NOTES:

_____

_____

_____

_____

_____

_____

_____

_____

_____

_____

_____

_____

_____

_____

_____

_____

FLOUR AND WATER FINGER PAINT

1 CUP FLOUR
1 CUP WATER
FOOD COLORING
OR 1 TABLESPOON POWDERED TEMPERA PAINT

1. Mix all the ingredients together in a bowl.
2. You can use the recipe to create several colors if you like. Add more food coloring to create vibrant colors, or put in a small amount for pastel colors.

HINTS: For young children learning primary colors, try making only one color at a time, or make two primary colors to create and learn about secondary colors (yellow and red make orange, etc). Does not store well. Try adding 1/4 cup salt for added texture and sparkle.

SUGGESTIONS: Cut an apple in half crosswise. Show children the star it makes inside. Use the apple to make paint prints on paper. Try cutting other fruits and vegetables: half of a strawberry (cut in half from stem to base), potato wedges, green peppers, star fruit, and orange wedges. Let your children have fun painting away!

NOTES:

_____

_____

_____

_____

_____

_____

_____

_____

_____

_____

_____

_____

_____

FRUIT SCENTED FINGER PAINT

1 1/8 CUP FLOUR
2 PACKETS UNSWEETENED DRINK MIX
1/2 CUP SALT
1 1/2 CUPS HOT WATER
1 1/2 TABLESPOONS COOKING OIL
FREEZER PAPER

1. Put all ingredients into a bowl.
2. Stir with wire whisk until well blended.
3. Paint on freezer paper.

HINTS: You can use this paint as a finger paint or as a brush paint. Paint on shiny side of freezer paper for wipe-away and start-over fun or paint on plain side for permanent art.

SUGGESTIONS: Johnny Appleseed once traveled around planting thousands of apple trees for settlers. Have your child paint scented orchards on a sheet of paper after reading the story about Johnny Appleseed's life. For variation ask the children what kind of fruit orchard or grape vineyard they would have planted. Have them paint a picture about it.

NOTES:

_____

_____

_____

_____

_____

_____

_____

_____

_____

_____

GELATIN FINGER PAINT

3 TABLESPOONS REGULAR FLAVORED GELATIN
3 TABLESPOONS LUKEWARM WATER
2 TABLESPOONS FLOUR

1. Mix all ingredients together until flour is no longer lumpy.
2. Put 2 tablespoons of paint on a piece of freezer paper, shiny side up, for children to create designs in over and over.
3. Air dry overnight.

HINTS: Try using the non-shiny side of freezer paper for another look or make two primary colors to create a secondary color. Use paint right away. Do not try to store in refrigerator.

SUGGESTIONS: Try this activity: Use 3 packets of flavored gelatin: cherry, orange, and lemon. Collect several different colored leaves from a variety of trees. Discuss how leaves change color in the fall. Tell the children to paint the leaves with their fingers on their paper. You will surely have a brightly colored fall picture!

NOTES:

_____

_____

_____

_____

_____

_____

_____

_____

_____

_____

_____

_____

LIQUID STARCH FINGER PAINT

LIQUID STARCH
POWDERED TEMPERA PAINT IN VARIOUS COLORS
CONSTRUCTION PAPER

1. Pour globs of liquid starch on construction paper.
2. Sprinkle a different color of tempera paint on each glob.
3. Use fingers to paint and create whatever you want!
4. Air dry.

HINTS: When doing finger painting with children, remember to put on smocks or old adult-size T-shirts. You can use surgical gloves or food handling gloves to lessen some of the mess. Have a great time!

SUGGESTIONS: Cut out magazine pictures that show different kinds of weather so that the children can look at them while they are painting. Explain to the children the different types of weather. When you are finished, have them sit down and finger paint their favorite type of weather.

NOTES:

_____

_____

_____

_____

_____

_____

_____

_____

_____

_____

NO MESS FINGER PAINT

1/4 CUP LIQUID LAUNDRY STARCH
3 TABLESPOONS POWDERED TEMPERA PAINT
1 LARGE AIRTIGHT PLASTIC BAG

1. Put liquid laundry starch in plastic bag.
2. Add powdered tempera paint.
3. Squeeze out the air before locking bag.
4. Seal tightly—you may want to secure bag with strong tape.
5. Squeeze bag to mix the starch and paint.
6. Lay plastic bag flat on table for child to use fingers and hands to make pictures on. Children will find they can erase and start over whenever they choose. Great for hours of non-messy fun!

SUGGESTIONS: I like this type of paint for working on alphabets and numbers because, like chalk, it is easily erasable. Shapes are lots of fun too. Have beginning writers practice tracing their names on these bags by printing their name on it in permanent black marker. They can take out the bag to practice whenever they want.

NOTES:

_____

_____

_____

_____

_____

_____

_____

_____

_____

_____

_____

WIPE AWAY SHAVING CREAM ART

1 CAN WHITE SHAVING CREAM
FOOD COLORING
PLASTIC EGG CARTON OR MEAT TRAYS

1. Spray blobs of shaving cream into egg carton sections or other suitable household item.
2. Add drops of a different food coloring to each section.
3. Stir with a plastic spoon.
4. Cover work area well. You can either allow children to work on tabletop or use wax paper, freezer paper, or construction paper. Great slippery fun!

HINTS: For larger groups of children try filling old Cool Whip containers with shaving cream and different food coloring mixtures. I recommend using smocks with this fun.

SUGGESTIONS: Children love smearing and mounding this fluffy paint. While working with the paint, ask them to tell you how it feels in their hands and what it smells like. Tell them to paint a picture of something that feels the same way. Another project to try is to make a picture of someone's pet. Talk about the different pets people have and how we take care of them.

NOTES:

_____

_____

_____

_____

_____

_____

_____

_____

_____

FACE PAINT

EASY FACE PAINT

1 TABLESPOON LIQUID TEMPERA PAINT
1 TEASPOON FACE LOTION
COTTON SWABS
SMALL CONTAINERS FOR MIXING
OR PLASTIC EGG CARTON

1. Combine tempera paint and face lotion.
2. Mix well.
3. Apply face paint with cotton swabs, sponges, or paintbrushes.
4. To remove, wash face with soap and water or with cleansing cream.

SUGGESTIONS: Discuss the many different jobs people do that involve some sort of stage makeup or face paint. Some are circus entertainers, clowns, actors, and makeup artists. Go to a play where the actors use a lot of makeup. Children can also make home-made face paint (p. 91) and see what animal faces they can create.

NOTES:

_____
_____
_____
_____
_____
_____
_____
_____
_____
_____
_____
_____
_____
_____

FACE AND BODY PAINT

3 TABLESPOONS SHORTENING
1 1/2 TABLESPOONS CORNSTARCH
FOOD COLORING
PAPER PLATE

1. In a small bowl mix shortening and cornstarch until smooth.
2. On a paper plate separate paint into 4 sections.
3. Add a few drops of food coloring to each one and mix until well blended.
4. Use a makeup sponge or Q-tips to apply.
5. Removes easily with a soapy washrag.

HINTS: You can add glitter to the paint for a sparkling effect.

SUGGESTIONS: Kids can use makeup on their wrists, feet, hands, arms, and face. See if they can make pretend jewelry on themselves or on a classmate. Get creative with designs.

NOTES:

_____

_____

_____

_____

_____

_____

_____

_____

_____

_____

_____

_____

HOMEMADE FACE PAINT

SMALL PAPER CUPS
6 TEASPOONS CORNSTARCH
3 TEASPOONS COLD CREAM
3 TEASPOONS WATER
FOOD COLORING
SMALL PAINTBRUSHES

1. To make six different colors put 1 teaspoon cornstarch, 1/2 teaspoon cold cream, 1/2 teaspoon water, and a few drops of food coloring in each paper cup.

2. Stir well to mix.

3. Dip brush in and start creating!

SUGGESTIONS: Many people around the world incorporate intricately painted facial designs into various aspects of their culture. Research and see what you can find out about one culture and its face-painting practices. Try to copy some of that culture's designs, and make up some of your own.

NOTES:

_____

_____

_____

_____

_____

_____

_____

_____

_____

_____

INK TYPE PAINT

COMIC COPIER

2 TEASPOONS VANILLA EXTRACT
2 TEASPOONS LIQUID DISH SOAP
NEWSPAPER COMICS
WHITE TYPING PAPER
PAINTBRUSH
SPOON

1. Mix vanilla extract and dish soap in a bowl.
2. Brush solution over comic with paintbrush.
3. Lay paper on top of comic and, using a spoon, press down on the picture, rubbing back and forth until the comic shows through.
4. Lift off the paper carefully, and you have a print of the comic.

SUGGESTIONS: This is a great way to make bookmarks and magnets. All you need is some white construction paper, a hole punch and string, contact paper, and sticky magnetic tape. Use clear contact paper to laminate the creations once they are dry. For a bookmark, punch a hole in the top with the hole punch and put the string through the hole. For a magnet, put a piece of sticky magnet tape on the back.

NOTES:

_____

_____

_____

_____

_____

_____

_____

_____

_____

_____

CRYSTALLIZED INK

3 TEASPOONS TABLE SALT
1/4 CUP WARM WATER
BLACK CONSTRUCTION PAPER
PAINTBRUSH OR COTTON SWABS

1. Mix table salt and warm water together and stir until dissolved.
2. Preheat oven to 150 degrees.
3. Use paintbrush or cotton swab to paint crystal ink on black paper.
4. Turn oven off and set paper in oven for 5 minutes.
5. Read message or see picture appear!

HINTS: Be sure to dip brush in salt solution each time to get a clear message.

SUGGESTIONS: Tell kids to make invisible messages or pictures for a friend or family member.

NOTES:

_____

_____

_____

_____

_____

_____

_____

_____

_____

_____

_____

EASY INVISIBLE INK

PURE LEMON JUICE
PAINTBRUSH OR COTTON SWAB
WHITE PAPER

1. Pour lemon juice into a dish.
2. Use paintbrush or cotton swab to write a message or draw a secret picture on white paper.
3. Let the picture or message dry.
4. To read, have an adult hold the paper over a heat source such as a toaster or a stove on low heat.
5. Your message will begin to appear as the heat turns the lemon juice brown.

SUGGESTIONS: Making messages that no one else can see is a lot of fun for the 7–10 age group. They will love drawing pictures for their friends. Tell them to watch how the lemon juice turns brown as it warms up. They will be amazed.

NOTES:

_____

_____

_____

_____

_____

_____

_____

_____

_____

_____

_____

_____

EDIBLE
FINGER PAINT

PUDDING FINGER PAINT

1 PACKAGE OF INSTANT VANILLA PUDDING
2 CUPS ICE COLD WATER (CHILL WATER IN FREEZER FOR 10–15 MINUTES)
FOOD COLORING (OPTIONAL)

1. Mix pudding with water using a wire whisk for 3 minutes.
2. Divide pudding into several bowls and add a different food coloring to each one.
3. Chill in refrigerator for 1 hour.
4. Allow children to paint on freezer paper and taste as they paint!

HINTS: Try this with tapioca for added texture. Just remember to add water instead of milk.

SUGGESTIONS: This is a fun, sticky paint that smells and tastes great. I like to use this paint to talk about the five senses. You can hear it move on the paper, it tastes sweet, it smells good, it looks colorful (if you add food coloring), and it feels cold and gooey. Have kids describe how everything seems to them.

NOTES:

_____

_____

_____

_____

_____

_____

_____

_____

_____

_____

_____

_____

_____

STICKY CORN SYRUP PAINT

1/4 CUP LIGHT CORN SYRUP
6–8 DROPS FOOD COLORING

1. Mix corn syrup and food coloring.
2. Stir until well blended.
3. Repeat steps for additional colors.

HINTS: Corn syrup paint is great sticky fun for little ones, but cover work surface well for easier cleanup. Poster board or thick paper works better than light-weight papers. Paintbrushes should be washed right away or set in water to soak. Artwork will need to dry overnight to create a nice glossy nonsticky picture. For added fun try adding glitter. FOR OLDER CHILDREN: create a nonedible paint using 1 tablespoon of powdered or liquid tempera paint for more vibrant colors. Store paint in an airtight container for reuse.

SUGGESTIONS: Learn about patterns with this recipe! Show children how to create different patterns with their fingers. Make a sample of dots and lines or dots of different colors. They will learn to see that if they put a combination of pictures together and alternate it, it will become a pattern.

NOTES:

_____

_____

_____

_____

_____

_____

_____

_____

_____

_____

TOAST PAINT

**WHITE BREAD SLICES
MILK
PAINTBRUSH**

1. Use milk to paint a design in the toast.
2. Pop bread into toaster on medium heat.
3. When the toast pops up, it will have a design on it.

SUGGESTIONS: Use this recipe to paint messages like "good morning" to children. Fun surprise messages help make reading fun. Little ones can make smiley faces and hearts to show you how they feel.

NOTES:

WHIPPED CREAM FINGER PAINT

1 CAN WHIPPED CREAM
FOOD COLORING

1. On freezer paper spray about a 1/2 cup of whipped cream and add a drop of food coloring.
2. With a spoon mix food coloring and whipped cream.
3. Let your child enjoy playing with this finger paint on freezer paper and tasting it.

HINTS: Try adding different food flavorings such as vanilla or orange extract.

SUGGESTIONS: Show children a picture of a rainbow. Make several colors of whipped cream finger paint and ask them to make their own rainbow.

NOTES:

_____

_____

_____

_____

_____

_____

_____

_____

_____

_____

_____

_____

_____

_____

_____

_____

OTHER PAINTS

BUBBLE PAINT

1 1/4 CUPS TEMPERA PAINT
1 3/4 CUPS DISH SOAP
1/8 CUP WATER
PLASTIC BOWL
DRINKING STRAW
WHITE PAPER
NEWSPAPER

1. Mix dish soap, tempera paint, and water in bowl. Cover table with newspaper.
2. Put straw in mixture and blow gently. Do not suck in!!
3. To capture bubble print, lay white paper on top of bubbles.
4. Press gently until bubbles start to pop.
5. Lift paper off to see the bubbles you captured!
6. Lay paper out to dry.
7. Have fun creating new masterpieces.

SUGGESTIONS: If you have an easel, try substituting food coloring for the tempera and blowing bubbles to the paper.

NOTES:

_____
_____
_____
_____
_____
_____
_____
_____
_____
_____

SIDEWALK PAINT

1/4 CUP CORNSTARCH
1/4 CUP COLD WATER
FOOD COLORING
LARGE PAINTBRUSH

1. Mix cornstarch and water together in a bowl.
2. Stir until well blended.
3. Add food coloring and mix again.
4. Repeat recipe until you have all the colors desired.

HINTS: This sidewalk paint washes off with water. Use cheap house painting brushes for wider strokes.

SUGGESTIONS: Use this sidewalk paint to make different traffic signs we see on the road, such as: slow, stop, yield, and children at play. Discuss what each sign means and what we do when we see them. Talk about looking both ways before crossing the road. A great way to learn life skills and safety rules. Sidewalk paint is also fun for big pictures being created by a group.

NOTES:

_____

_____

_____

_____

_____

_____

_____

_____

_____

SQUEEZE CHALK

1/2 CUP CORNSTARCH
3 1/2 TABLESPOONS FLOUR
1/2 CUP WATER
1 TABLESPOON POWDERED TEMPERA
FREEZER BAG

1. Put all ingredients in a plastic freezer bag.
2. Using a long-handled spoon, stir mixture until well blended.
3. Seal bag.
4. Cut a small corner of the bag to create a tip.
5. Repeat for a variety of colors.

HINTS: Add glitter for sparkling effect.

SUGGESTIONS: Squeeze chalk is great for drawing on the sidewalk, heavy poster board, or cardboard. Ask kids to use their chalk to make a picture of what they want to do when they grow up. It can be an object used at that job, a person, or a place. Have them tell you all about it.

NOTES:

_____

_____

_____

_____

_____

_____

_____

_____

_____

_____

WATERCOLOR POPS

1/2 CUP WATER
2 TEASPOONS POWDERED TEMPERA PAINT
POPSICLE STICKS
ICE CUBE TRAY OR DIXIE CUPS
WAX PAPER

1. Mix paint and water together in a bowl.
2. Pour the mixture into Dixie cups or ice cube tray.
3. Cover the cups with squares of wax paper and insert Popsicle sticks. Or cover ice cube tray with plastic wrap and insert Popsicle sticks.
4. Freeze until frozen solid.
5. Remove watercolor pops from cup or tray.
6. Dip the frozen watercolor pop in water to get it going and start painting.

HINTS: It is easier to remove the watercolor pops if you first run them under warm water for a few seconds.

SUGGESTIONS: Use watercolor pops to make wrapping paper for gifts or book covers.

NOTES:

_____

_____

_____

_____

_____

_____

_____

_____

_____

_____

Part 3:
Pastes and Glues

PASTES

COOKED PASTE

1/2 CUP CORNSTARCH
2 TABLESPOONS SUGAR
1 CUP COLD WATER
1/2 TEASPOON MINT EXTRACT

1. Mix cornstarch and sugar in a cooking pot.
2. Gradually add cold water until smooth.
3. Cook over medium heat until mixture resembles paste. DO NOT OVERCOOK.
4. Add 1/2 teaspoon of mint extract and mix well.
5. Cool before using.

SUGGESTIONS: Offer children a stack of old magazines and age-appropriate scissors. Set the paste on the table. Have the children make collages of different pictures to reflect the different feelings we have and the things that make us happy or sad. Other collage themes to try: fall, winter, spring, summer, things we like to do, beautiful places, animals, trees, food groups (do one at a time), and shapes.

NOTES:

_____
_____
_____
_____
_____
_____
_____
_____
_____
_____
_____

COTTON SCULPTING PASTE

1 CUP FLOUR
1 CUP WATER
1 BAG COTTON BALLS
ALUMINUM FOIL

1. Mix flour and water in a bowl until it forms a pastelike mixture.
2. Place aluminum foil on a baking sheet.
3. Dip cotton balls in paste until well coated on all sides. Place dipped cotton balls on foil to make different shapes and creations.
4. Bake in oven at 325 degrees for 20–60 minutes until hard and lightly browned.
5. Cool for 10 minutes, then carefully peel off sculpture.

HINTS: Try using dryer lint instead of cotton balls. Make sure that all sides are completely coated with paste. You can add glitter to the paste or paint the creation after it has been baked and cooled. If you want only one color, add food coloring to paste.

SUGGESTIONS: Ideas for sculpting: caterpillars, butterflies, giraffes, snakes, snails, slugs, ants, spiders, alphabets, numbers, angels, snowmen, stars. When all else fails, use your imagination.

NOTES:

_____
_____
_____
_____
_____
_____
_____
_____

FLOUR AND WATER PASTE

2 CUPS FLOUR
1 CUP WATER
PLASTIC BAG

1. Mix the flour and water together until you get a sticky mixture.
2. Add 1 extra tablespoon of water if paste appears too thick.

HINTS: If mixture dries out, add a little more water and mix well. This is a safe mixture for little ones who put their fingers in their mouth. It is a great quick fix if you need paste. Store paste in an airtight plastic bag in refrigerator.

SUGGESTIONS: Have shapes cut out of paper ahead of time, making sure there are several for each child. Toddlers and preschoolers are just learning about pasting. Set out the paste with some large craft sticks and a sheet of paper for each child. Demonstrate how to put the paste on the back of the shape and then stick it to the paper. Talk about the shapes as they glue them.

NOTES:

_____
_____
_____
_____
_____
_____
_____
_____
_____
_____
_____
_____
_____

HEAVY DUTY PASTE MIX

1 1/2 TABLESPOON CORNSTARCH
1/8 CUP WHITE GLUE

1. Mix cornstarch and glue until smooth.
2. Spread with craft sticks.

HINTS: If paste hardens, add a few drops of water and mix well. Store in airtight container. Use within one week for best results.

SUGGESTIONS: Use this paste mixture to make structures like houses, barns, bridges, buildings, churches, and playgrounds. Encourage kids to use their imaginations. Give them a variety of materials to work with, such as buttons, sticks, string, pipe cleaners, lids, etc. These projects are good for two-person teams. Children will learn about working together and will see that it takes a lot of people to make the large buildings we see every day.

NOTES:

_____
_____
_____
_____
_____
_____
_____
_____
_____
_____
_____
_____
_____

GLUES

AWESOME GLITTER GLUE

3/4 CUP WATER
1 TEASPOON WHITE VINEGAR
2 TABLESPOONS CORN SYRUP
1/2 CUP CORNSTARCH
3/4 CUP COLD WATER
1 1/2 TABLESPOONS GLITTER

1. In a pot stir water, corn syrup, and vinegar until smooth.
2. In a bowl stir cornstarch and cold water together. Set aside.
3. Heat the water, corn syrup, and vinegar mixture over medium heat until it boils.
4. Slowly add the cornstarch mixture, stirring until well blended. It will look like soft pudding.
5. Remove from heat and add glitter.
6. Allow mixture to cool before storing in an airtight squeeze bottle.
7. Let the glue sit overnight before using.

HINTS: For airtight squeeze bottles, you can use old mustard containers, ketchup bottles, or recycled washed glue bottles. Try adding a drop of food coloring for extra sparkle!

SUGGESTIONS: Use this glue for making string art collages. Have several types and colors of string on a table. Allow children to be imaginative with the pictures they can make out of their string. The glitter in the glue will make a nice sparkling effect. They can try this with colored noodles as well.

NOTES:

_____
_____
_____
_____
_____
_____

EGG WHITE GLUE

EGG WHITE
PAINTBRUSH

1. Separate yolk from egg white.
2. Brush egg white onto lightweight items such as kite paper, typing paper, or plastic (like a garbage bag).

HINTS: This is a cheap glue that is strong and weightless.

NOTES:

_____

_____

_____

_____

_____

_____

_____

_____

_____

_____

_____

_____

_____

_____

_____

_____

_____

GELATIN STICKER GLUE

2 TABLESPOONS BOILING WATER
1 TABLESPOON FLAVORED GELATIN
SMALL PICTURES
BOWL
PAINTBRUSH

1. Mix boiling water and gelatin together in bowl.
2. Brush mixture onto the back of pictures with paintbrush.
3. Let pictures dry sticky side up.
4. When stickers dry, lick the sticky side and stick away.

SUGGESTIONS: Take a sheet of typing paper or file folder and coat the back with the sticker glue. Let dry and cut into different shapes. Have kids draw and color their own stickers and fake stamps.

NOTES:

_____
_____
_____
_____
_____
_____
_____
_____
_____
_____
_____
_____
_____

Part 4:
Other Fun Stuff

SAND CONCOCTIONS

COLORED SAND MIX

1/2 CUP DRY SAND
2 TABLESPOONS POWDERED TEMPERA PAINT
THINNED WHITE GLUE (2 PARTS GLUE TO 1 PART WATER)
SMALL BOWLS

1. Mix sand and powdered tempera.
2. Repeat recipe for each desired color.
3. Use separate bowls for each color.
4. Use the thinned glue to paint sections of a picture at a time, then pour the desired color on.

HINTS: This can be done outside on nice days. For less mess and quicker storage use plastic bags for mixing, then pour out what you will need onto recycled meat trays. Use spoons for scooping sand onto picture.

SUGGESTIONS: Supply children with a large sheet of white paper and ask them to draw a picture of a child. Ask them to draw clothes on the child. When they are done with that, set out the colors of sand and ask them to color in the child's clothes. Talk about what kind of clothes we wear when it is sunny, rainy, snowy, or windy.

NOTES:

_____

_____

_____

_____

_____

_____

_____

_____

_____

_____

3-D SAND PAINT

1/3 CUP FLOUR
1/3 CUP WATER
1/3 CUP SALT
1 TABLESPOON DRY SAND
2 1/2 TABLESPOONS POWDERED TEMPERA PAINT
1 TABLESPOON LIQUID WHITE GLUE
QUART SIZE PLASTIC BAGS
POSTER BOARD

1. Combine dry ingredients in a bowl.
2. Add water and paint. Mix well.
3. Spoon mixture into plastic baggies, seal, and cut off a small portion of one bottom corner.
4. Repeat process to create as many colors as you like.
5. Create original artwork by squeezing sand paint from corner of baggie onto heavy paper.
6. Let finished artwork dry 24 hours or until hard.

HINTS: Try using a cake decorating funnel for sand paint rather than bags. You can add glitter for some really sparkly artwork.

SUGGESTIONS: Kids can have a great time creating scenes on poster board. Poster board can also be used to make greeting cards. At your local craft store you will find cardboard picture frames on which children can create their own personal designs. Makes a great gift for Mother's Day or Father's Day!

NOTES:
_____
_____
_____
_____

EASY SAND CASTLE CLAY

4 CUPS SAND
2 CUPS CORNSTARCH
3 CUPS LIQUID CORNSTARCH

1. Combine sand and cornstarch in an old pot.
2. Add liquid starch and mix.
3. Cook over medium heat, constantly stirring until mixture thickens to a doughlike consistency.
4. Remove from heat and let cool for 5 minutes.
5. Knead for 1 minute.
6. Build sand castles on cardboard.
7. Allow to dry until hard.

HINTS: Try adding 1 tablespoon of powdered tempera paint to the mixture before cooling it. Or you can paint castles when they are completely dry,

SUGGESTIONS: Instead of molding sand castles, try molding an airplane or a pirate ship.

NOTES:

_____

_____

_____

_____

_____

_____

_____

_____

_____

_____

_____

SALTY SAND MIX

1 CUP SALT
2 TABLESPOONS POWDERED TEMPERA PAINT
ZIPLOC BAGS

1. Pour salt and tempera paint into plastic bag.
2. Shake bag until color is well blended.
3. Repeat the steps until you have several colors of salty sand.

HINTS: Store leftover sand in Ziploc bags.

SUGGESTIONS: Use salt sand with a clear bottle to create bottle art projects. Alternate colors to create a cool design in the bottle. Or have children outline a picture with white school glue and sprinkle salty sand over the glue to create a raised picture.

NOTES:

_____
_____
_____
_____
_____
_____
_____
_____
_____
_____
_____
_____
_____
_____

SAND CASTLES

PASTE MIXTURE:
1/2 CUP FLOUR
2 TABLESPOONS SUGAR
3/4 CUP WATER

CASTLE RECIPE:
6 CUPS DRY SAND
1 CUP PASTE MIXTURE

ADDITIONAL ITEMS NEEDED:
PAINT (OPTIONAL), CONTAINERS FOR CASTLE BUILDING
SPOON, BUTTER KNIFE (FOR CARVING), CARDBOARD OR PLYWOOD FOR BASE

1. Make paste by mixing ingredients in a bowl until lumps are gone.
2. Mix castle recipe by mixing dry sand and paste mixture.
3. Add a little extra water until mixture will pack into containers firmly. Begin creating castle on heavy cardboard or plywood base.
4. Let the castle dry 1–3 days. Larger projects will take longer to dry. Place castle in an undisturbed place for drying. It will fall apart if poked before completely drying.

HINTS: You may clear coat your castle with clear acrylic hobby coating or spray with clear enamel in a well-ventilated area. Create castles using various objects such as cans, cottage cheese cups, yogurt containers, small buckets, paper cups of various sizes, Styrofoam cups, etc. Suggested items to accessorize your castle: beads, buttons, flags, sequins, shells, craft sticks, glitter, etc. I would use this project for older children because it requires a lot of patience. I found that it can take several days to dry and is not completely rock hard. It offers a lot of challenge, since you need to be careful not to disturb the castle. When dry, you can paint it if you like.

SUGGESTIONS: Try molding mixture around a can and drying for a volcano. If mixture is too runny, add a little more flour. You can create sand drizzle art with the runny mix.

NOTES:
_____
_____
_____
_____

SAND MODELING

1 CUP OF DRY SAND
1/2 CUP CORNSTARCH
3/4 CUP HOT WATER
1/2 TABLESPOON ALUM
FOOD COLORING (OPTIONAL)

1. Mix all ingredients in a pot.
2. Cook on medium heat until mixture forms a thick dough.
3. Model as desired.
4. Air dry 3–4 days, depending on size.

HINTS: Begins to dry quickly. I recommend using an old pot for cooking. Double or triple the recipe for bigger projects. Makes a great group project.

SUGGESTIONS: Try making these projects: castles, dragons, rocks, roads for toy cars, bridges, mountains, etc.

NOTES:

_____

_____

_____

_____

_____

_____

_____

_____

_____

_____

_____

_____

SENSORY RECIPES
FOR FUN

COLORED RICE, SAND, OR NOODLES

1/4 CUP RUBBING ALCOHOL
FOOD COLORING
1/2 CUP OF CLEAN SAND OR RICE OR NOODLES
ZIPLOC BAGS
SIEVE

1. Mix rubbing alcohol with several drops of food coloring in plastic bag.
2. Add sand, rice, or noodles. Squish bag until contents are completely colored.
3. Let sand sit for 15–20 minutes. Let rice or noodles sit for 5–8 minutes.
4. Drain rice or noodles through sieve over the sink or into a bucket or can.
5. Spread over an area covered with newspaper or old towels to dry. Let dry for at least 1 hour. This will ensure that the alcohol has evaporated and the product is safe for kids to handle.

HINTS: Store in medium- or large-sized containers.

SUGGESTIONS: Have kids make jewelry such as bracelets and necklaces by stringing noodles with holes on colored yarn. Sand can be used as a paint medium by applying glue, then sprinkling sand over it and letting it dry. Also can use as a sensory experience for children by letting them use sieves, measuring cups, spoons, and small containers for filling and spilling.

NOTES:

_____

_____

_____

_____

_____

_____

_____

FIREWORKS ART

MILK
FOOD COLORING
PLATE
TOOTHPICK OR COTTON SWAB
DISH SOAP

1. Pour enough milk on the plate to cover completely.
2. Drip drops of different food colorings into the milk.
3. Dip a toothpick or cotton swab in dish soap, then put in the middle of food coloring drops.
4. Watch the food coloring swirl with firework color!

SUGGESTIONS: Use this as a discussion project. Ask the children what they see happening and ask them to tell you why they think it happened.

NOTES:

_____

_____

_____

_____

_____

_____

_____

_____

_____

_____

_____

_____

_____

FLUBBER

2 CUPS WHITE GLUE
1 1/2 CUPS WATER
FOOD COLORING
1 1/3 CUPS WATER
3 TEASPOONS BORAX LAUNDRY SOAP
TWO BOWLS

1. In one bowl mix together glue, water, and food coloring.
2. In the other bowl mix water and Borax.
3. Pour both mixtures together. Don't mix. Instead, pull up gently with hands. At first it will be stringy. Knead and pull until all the liquid has been absorbed.
4. Have fun playing with flubber. It will become more pliable as you play with it and it warms up.

HINTS: Flubber stores well in an airtight container in the refrigerator. Play over a covered area.

SUGGESTIONS: Flubber gives opportunity for a great hands-on discussion of science. Ask children to test if it bounces, if it keeps shape, and if it melts. Ask them to tell you how it feels. Is it cold? Put it in the refrigerator for 1 hour and see what happens. Does it break apart? Flubber is a lot of fun because children can't decide if it is a solid or a liquid. It really gets them thinking. I used this recipe at an open house for the preschool I worked for. The parents and children loved it. I remember the parents' amazement when they discovered that I had made it.

NOTES:

_____

_____

_____

_____

_____

GOOBLEK

1 CUP CORNSTARCH
1/2 CUP WATER
PLASTIC STORAGE CONTAINER
SPOON
FOOD COLORING (OPTIONAL)
PLASTIC COVERING FOR TABLE
(for easier cleanup)

1. Pour cornstarch and water in pan or plastic container.
2. Mix well. Add food coloring if desired.
3. Play with gooblek with hands and have a messy fun time!

HINTS: Do not pour down drain. Dispose of in trash can. Gooblek does not store well in airtight container. Leave lid off and, as water evaporates, add more water to reuse.

SUGGESTIONS: Another great discussion concoction! This one is interesting to children because it hardens if they squeeze it, and it's a liquid if they don't. Have older children experiment with the recipe and write down what they discover.

NOTES:

_____

_____

_____

_____

_____

_____

_____

_____

_____

_____

PUTTY

2 TABLESPOONS LIQUID STARCH
4 TABLESPOONS WHITE GLUE
FOOD COLORING (OPTIONAL)
SMALL PLASTIC CONTAINER

1. Mix white glue and food coloring (optional) together in a bowl.
2. Pour liquid starch into another bowl.
3. Pour the glue mixture on top of the liquid starch.
4. Allow mixture to sit for 3–4 minutes.
5. Stir first with a spoon, then knead. It will be gooey at first but continue kneading until it is a smooth putty.

HINTS: Use caution, as this is difficult to get out of carpet. Have children sit at a table. As a surprise gift put in a plastic Easter egg. Do not press on paper, as it will stick. Very sticky and slimy feeling, but kids love it. Store in an airtight container.

SUGGESTIONS: Use this as free exploration. Make one batch of flubber (p. 139) and one batch of putty. Ask children to tell you if they see any differences between the two. Check to see if one bounces and the other doesn't, or see what happens when you stretch them if they are cold or warm.

NOTES:

THE SENSORY BUCKET

Children enjoy all kinds of hands-on fun. The sensory bucket provides just that, along with plenty of exploration and learning. All you need to do is collect a few household items and a storage container with a lid. A five-gallon container or larger is suitable. Kids will explore measuring, textures, volumes, scooping, sink and float, and pouring.

Below, you will find plenty of ideas for filling your sensory bucket and also some ideas for the kind of household items with which to equip it.

SENSORY BUCKET FILLERS

brown rice, white rice (colored or plain),
oatmeal, noodles (various types and colors),
cornmeal, sand, salt, sawdust, shredded paper,
good old-fashioned dirt, water and shells, beans (one kind or a variety),
flaxseed, grass seed, bird seed, chicken scratch (feed stores),
potting soil, pea gravel, wheat germ, grits, cheerios, popcorn seeds

MATERIALS TO ADD TO WATER SENSORY BUCKET

In the water sensory bucket add shells and rocks. Give children sponges and toothbrushes for washing them. You can also give them little plastic boats, squeeze bottles, and basters. Give them items for sink and float experiments. Here is a list of ideas: rocks, pencils, spoons, marbles (plastic and glass), feathers, nuts, rubber balls, pieces of wood. In addition to these ideas, look around the house and see what else you can come up with.

EQUIPMENT FOR DRY SENSORY BUCKET

In the dry sensory bucket give children any variety of these items: small cars, cups, funnels, spoons, small bowls, measuring cups, plastic experiment tubes, small plastic juice pitchers, washed pudding cups, weight scale, and recycled frozen juice containers.

NOTES:
_____
_____
_____
_____
_____

BUBBLES

BASIC BUBBLE RECIPE

1 1/2 CUPS WATER
1/2 CUP LIQUID DISH SOAP
1/4 CUP GLYCERIN
1/2 TEASPOON CORN SYRUP

1. Mix all ingredients in a dishpan or baking pan.
2. Allow mixture to rest overnight.
3. Use straws, hangers, or store-bought bubble wands to blow your bubbles. Enjoy!

HINTS: This recipe can be doubled for larger groups.

SUGGESTIONS: For older children, try experimenting with the quantities of the ingredients. See if varied recipes create more bubbles or bigger bubbles or if they make any bubbles at all.

NOTES:

_____
_____
_____
_____
_____
_____
_____
_____
_____
_____
_____
_____
_____
_____

GIANT BUBBLE SOLUTION

THIN WIRE
1 BOTTLE BUBBLE-BLOWING LIQUID
2 TABLESPOONS GLYCERIN
2 TABLESPOONS DISHWASHING LIQUID

1. Mix all ingredients together in a shallow bowl or baking pan.
2. With the wire, shape a giant loop up to 10 inches in diameter. Twist wire around base of wand to hold.
3. Dip your new bubble wand into the solution.
4. Don't blow, just wave your wand around in the air to make mega bubbles.

SUGGESTIONS: Try shaping the wire into other shapes such as a square or diamond and see what happens. Use straws with cut ends, plastic six-pack holders, paper cups with the bottoms cut out, a funnel, a plastic hanger, or an Easter egg holder. Kids will have fun deciding which items make the best bubble blowers.

NOTES:

_____

_____

_____

_____

_____

_____

_____

_____

_____

_____

_____

_____

_____

QUICK BLOWING BUBBLES

1/4 CUP JOY DISHWASHING SOAP
1/2-3/4 CUP WATER
1 TEASPOON SUGAR
A FEW DROPS FOOD COLORING (OPTIONAL)

1. In a shallow bowl gently mix soap, sugar, and coloring. Slowly add 1/2 cup water and gently stir. If too thick add remaining water.
2. For best results, let the bubble solution sit for a few days to age.

HINTS: An old bubble container or Tupperware container is great for storing unused bubble solution.

SUGGESTIONS: You can often find bubble wands for sale separately at learning stores, party stores, or toy stores. Look around the house to see what you have handy and create your own bubble wands.

NOTES:

PAPER-MACHE

HELPFUL HINTS FOR PAPER-MACHE

Paper-mache is a fun project for children. The steps required to complete this project are a little complex for younger children. Doing a project like paper-mache can create awesome results but can take several days to complete. Keep in mind the age of the children you are working with when doing the project. Fun projects for children may include making vases, mugs, planters, or masks. Under each recipe is a suggestion that can be mixed with any of the recipes to see what you like best.

BASES FOR PAPER-MACHE

Bases for paper-mache models may be balloons, jars, inflatable figures, balls, or wire frames. Older children can even use light bulbs, with caution, of course. Other objects to try are tin cans, coffee cans, old plates, old bowls, ice cream cartons, paper towel tubes, aluminum foil, cardboard, paper cups, plastic tubs, or a paper bag filled with paper for a full head mask. Try using paper-mache for relief maps by bunching up newspaper and taping it onto a cardboard base. Glue or tape cut-out cardboard or heavy paper for ears, legs, etc. When using paper-mache on an object that needs to be removed, first oil or grease the object with petroleum jelly or liquid soap so it will slip off easily.

COVERINGS

Paper-mache strips can be newspaper, construction paper, crepe paper, tissue paper, napkins, etc. Try streamers. Experiment to see what you like best.

DRYING

Allow project to air dry for best results. Heating up the object tends to make it shrink and buckle. Set project near heat vent or in a sunny window. Apply four to five layers and dry overnight, then add a few more layers. This will prevent molding.

BEFORE PAINTING

Sanding the finished paper-mache project can give it a smoother finish before painting. Use fine to medium sandpaper.

PAINTING

If you're using tempera paint, give it an undercoat of gesso or thinned white latex paint. Tempera painted projects should be sprayed with a clear plastic finish or clear varnish for protection. Acrylic paint does not require a base coat.

OTHER TIPS

Be sure to thoroughly protect the work area by covering with plastic garbage bags, a tarp, or newspapers. This is a fun project but tends to be messy. To eliminate messy fingers I suggest food handlers gloves or surgical latex gloves. I also recommend that you cover your clothes with an old shirt or smock.

STORAGE OR DISPOSAL

Store unused portion of paper-mache in an airtight container in the refrigerator for only one or two days or dump in the garbage. Do not dispose of in garbage disposals or sinks.

EASY PAPER-MACHE

2 CUPS LIQUID STARCH
NEWSPAPER STRIPS

1. Pour 2 cups of liquid starch in a bowl.
2. Use finger to apply to newspaper strips, wiping off excess.
3. Apply several layers to project. Allow to dry 24 hours, then apply several more layers.
4. Allow finished project to dry 2–3 days, maybe more depending on size and the number of layers of mache.
5. Paint or decorate.

HINTS: Use this mixture for older children, since it is a chemical.

SUGGESTIONS: Make a garbage can by greasing the outside of a small garbage can. Put on several layers of paper-mache. Allow to dry overnight. Coat with several more layers of paper-mache. Allow to dry. Paint project and spray with a clear coat.

NOTES:

_____

_____

_____

_____

_____

_____

_____

_____

_____

_____

_____

_____

LINT MACHE

3 CUPS DRYER LINT
2 CUPS WARM WATER
2/3 CUP WHEAT FLOUR

1. Mix all ingredients in a pot on the stove.
2. Stir well over medium heat until mixture begins to thicken and stick together.
3. Pour out onto newspaper to cool.
4. Mold over bottles, canning jars, boxes, and balloons.
5. Dries in 2–3 days, depending on project.

HINTS: Paint project with poster paint or watered-down acrylic paint, then coat it with shellac or clear spray for protection. Dry well before painting.

SUGGESTIONS: Have fun creating cool gift boxes and vases, or try molding into critters. To make pencil/pen holders, shape over canning jars.

NOTES:

_____

_____

_____

_____

_____

_____

_____

_____

_____

_____

_____

_____

NO COOK PAPER-MACHE

2 CUPS COLD WATER
1 1/2 – 1 3/4 CUPS FLOUR
NEWSPAPER STRIPS

1. In a large bowl mix water and flour with a wire whisk until smooth, but not too thick.
2. Coat a mold with one layer of newspaper that has been dipped in water only.
3. Next, dip strips into goop and layer over first layer until several layers have been applied.
4. Dry 1–2 days. Then apply additional layers. Allow to thoroughly dry 2–3 days or more, depending on project.
5. Paint or decorate if desired.

HINTS: This is a good beginner paper-mache recipe. It is quick to prepare. Show children how to wipe off excess goop.

SUGGESTIONS: Have children cover a balloon to make a piggy bank. Tape on cardboard ears and legs and use a pipe cleaner for a squiggly tail. Cover cardboard and balloon with a second layer of paper-mache. When finished, cut a slit in the top with a knife. Kids can break open piggy bank when full.

NOTES:

_____

_____

_____

_____

_____

_____

_____

_____

PAPER-MACHE GOO

1/2 CUP WHITE FLOUR
2 CUPS WATER
GLASS BOWL

1. In a pot, stir water and flour together until there are no lumps.
2. Cook over medium heat, stirring until mixture boils. Continue to cook for 10 seconds.
3. Remove from heat and cool
4. Use for paper-mache projects.

SUGGESTIONS: Tape together three different-sized balloons to make a snowman. Use a piece of paper in the shape of a cone to make a nose and pieces of tinfoil rolled in a ball to make eyes and a mouth. Cover with several layers of paper-mache. Paint when completely dried.

NOTES:

_____

_____

_____

_____

_____

_____

_____

_____

_____

_____

_____

_____

_____

PAPER-MACHE MIXTURE

4 CUPS FLOUR
1 CUP SUGAR
1 GALLON WARM WATER
1 QUART COLD WATER
OLD NEWSPAPERS

1. In a large pot, mix flour, sugar, and enough of the warm water to make a smooth paste.
2. Gradually add the remainder of the warm water.
3. Bring mixture to a boil and stir until thick and clear.
4. Take off stove top and thin with one quart of cold water.
5. Tear newspapers into long strips.
6. Pull strip through paste and squeeze off excess with fingers.
7. Cover your base or model with the strips all facing in the same direction.
8. Apply a second layer of strips, running the opposite of the first layer. Continue until four or five layers have been applied.
9. Allow to dry thoroughly. This can take 1–2 days or up to a week.

HINTS: This mixture is best if used right away or within a day or two. Always store in an airtight container.

SUGGESTIONS: Use an empty laundry detergent box with the lid still attached to make a treasure box. Tape a piece of cardboard about 6 inches by 2 inches for a handle. Cover with paper-mache. Allow to dry and coat again. After it is dry, paint and decorate with fake jewels from a craft store.

NOTES:

_____

_____

_____

_____

PULP MACHE

TORN NEWSPAPER IN 1 INCH SQUARES
2 CUPS WATER
1/2 CUP FLOUR
1 TABLESPOON WHITE GLUE
1 CUP SOAKED NEWSPAPER

1. Fill a quart jar with torn newspaper pieces. Cover with water and let it sit overnight.
2. Squeeze out excess water. Put water, flour, and glue in blender.
3. Add one cup of the pulped newspaper.
4. Turn on blender and blend well!
5. Your pulp mache is ready to use.

SUGGESTIONS: For vases or planters mold on outside of tin cans. For masks mold over paper bags stuffed with paper. Allow up to 1 week to dry. Sand off rough edges before painting if desired.

NOTES:

_____

_____

_____

_____

_____

_____

_____

_____

_____

_____

_____

_____

WHERE TO FIND INGREDIENTS

ACRYLIC PAINTS: tubes or small containers in craft stores or in craft aisle in general department stores.

ALUM: spice section in grocery stores.

BORAX: laundry detergent aisle of grocery stores.

CLEAR VARNISH OR ENAMEL: craft or hardware stores.

CONFETTI: party and craft stores.

CRAFT STICKS: craft stores.

CREAM OF TARTAR: spice section in grocery stores.

DECORATIVE MARBLES: garden nurseries, garden department of hardware stores, and craft stores.

GLYCERIN: pharmacies or drug stores.

LATEX GLOVES: pharmacies or drug stores.

PAINTBRUSHES: craft or hardware stores.

PASTE FOOD COLORING: baking section of craft stores.

RUBBING ALCOHOL: first aid section of grocery or drug stores.

SANDBOX SAND: larger toy stores or hardware stores.

SAWDUST: lumber department of hardware stores (they will usually give it to you for free). A friend or relative who does woodworking usually has lots around they would enjoy getting rid of.

SHELLAC: craft stores and hardware stores.

SPONGES: craft stores.

TEMPERA PAINT: powered or liquid can be found in craft stores.

TOASTED WHEAT GERM: cereal section of grocery stores.

TUMBLED SEA GLASS: garden nurseries, garden department of hardware stores, and craft stores.

WHITE GLUE: extra large, economical containers can be bought at hardware stores.

ABOUT THE AUTHOR

Selena LaPorte lives in Washington state with her husband and two sons. As a pre-school teacher who loved to challenge her students with sticky, messy projects, she saw the need for one comprehensive book of recipes for the stuff that makes learning fun. This book is the result of her extensive research and thorough testing.